The Five Senses

Tasting

Rebecca Rissman

Heinemann Library
Chicago, Illinois

www.heinemannraintree.com
Visit our website to find out more information about Heinemann-Raintree books.

To order:

☎ Phone 888-454-2279

🖳 Visit www.heinemannraintree.com to browse our catalog and order online.

Edited by Rebecca Rissman and Catherine Veitch
Designed by Ryan Frieson and Kimberly R. Miracle
Original illustrations © Capstone Global Library
Illustrated by Tony Wilson (pp. 11, 22)
Picture research by Tracy Cummins
Originated by Heinemann Library
Printed in China by South China Printing Company Ltd

14 13 12 11 10
10 9 8 7 6 5 4 3 2 1

Library of Congress Cataloging-in-Publication Data
Tasting / Rebecca Rissman.
p. cm. -- (The five senses)
ISBN 978-1-4329-3683-9 (hc) -- ISBN 978-1-4329-3689-1 (pb)
QP456.R57 2010
612.8'7--dc22
2009022290

Acknowledgments
The author and publishers are grateful to the following for permission to reproduce copyright material: Alamy p. 21 (© Andrew Fox); Corbis pp. 7 (© Don Mason), 10 (© Heide Benser); Getty Images pp. 6 (ABSODELS), 12 (Eric Millette), 13 (Robert Warren), 14 (Bambu Productions), 16 (Robert Daly), 17 (AE Pictures Inc.); istockphoto p. 8 (alvarez); Photolibrary p. 18 (Digital Vision); Shutterstock pp. 4 (© Sergey Pristyazhnyuk), 5 (© topal), 9 (© Victor Newman), 15 (© Monkey Business Images), 19 (© goldenangel), 20 (© nateperro), 23 A (© goldenangel), 23 B (© topal), 23 C (© Victor Newman), 23D (© nateperro).

Cover photograph of a boy eating a watermelon reproduced with permission of Getty Images (ColorBlind Images). Back cover photograph of a girl eating meat reproduced with permission of Shutterstock (© nateperro).

The publishers would like to thank Nancy Harris, Yael Biederman, and Matt Siegel for their assistance in the preparation of this book.

Every effort has been made to contact copyright holders of any material reproduced in this book. Any omissions will be rectified in subsequent printings if notice is given to the publisher.

Contents

Senses. 4

How Do You Taste? 8

What Do You Taste? 14

Naming the Parts
 You Use to Taste. 22

Picture Glossary 23

Index 24

Senses

We all have five senses.

We use our senses every day.

Tasting and smelling are senses.

Seeing, hearing, and touching are also senses.

How Do You Taste?

mouth

You use your mouth to taste.

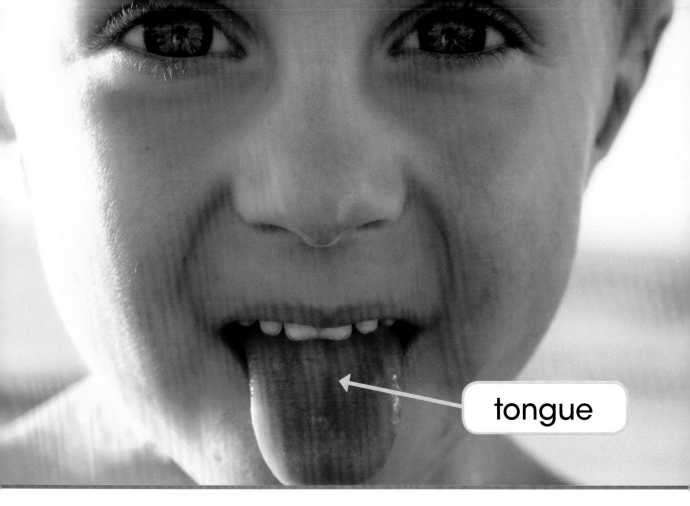

tongue

Your tongue helps you to taste.

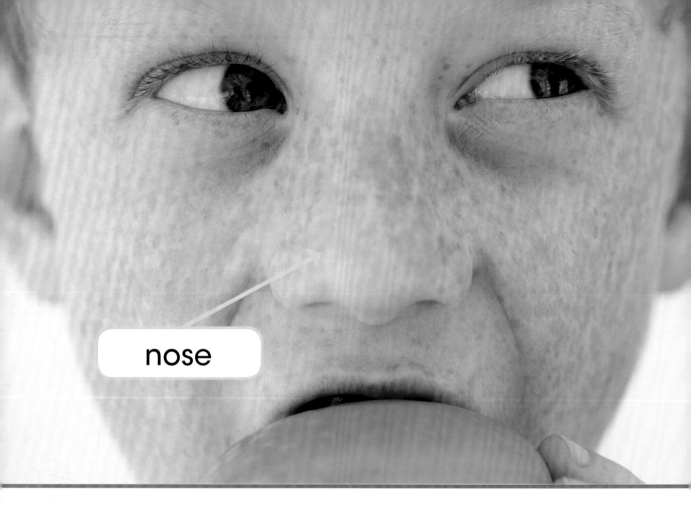

nose

You use your nose to smell.

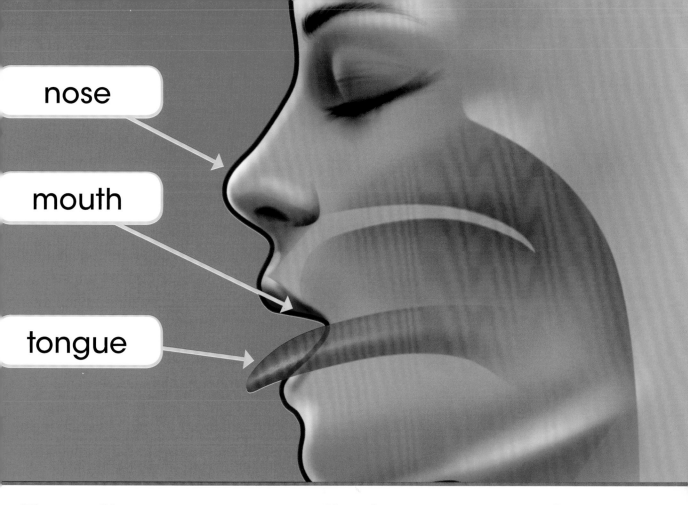

nose

mouth

tongue

Together your mouth, tongue, and
nose help you to taste.

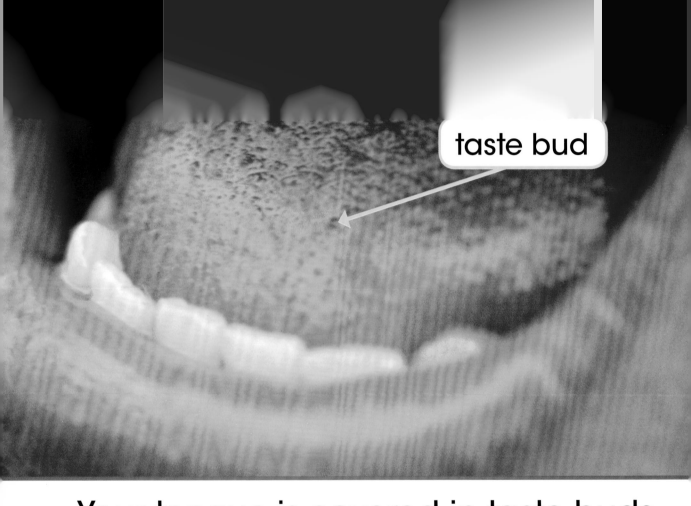

Your tongue is covered in taste buds.

Taste buds help you taste
different things.

What Do You Taste?

You can taste food and drinks.

You can taste five main flavors.

You can taste sour flavors. Lemons taste sour.

You can taste bitter flavors. Olives taste bitter.

You can taste salty flavors. Popcorn tastes salty.

You can taste sweet flavors. Fruit tastes sweet.

You can taste umami flavors. Umami
is a meaty flavor.

You can taste many flavors at the same time.

Naming the Parts
You Use to Taste

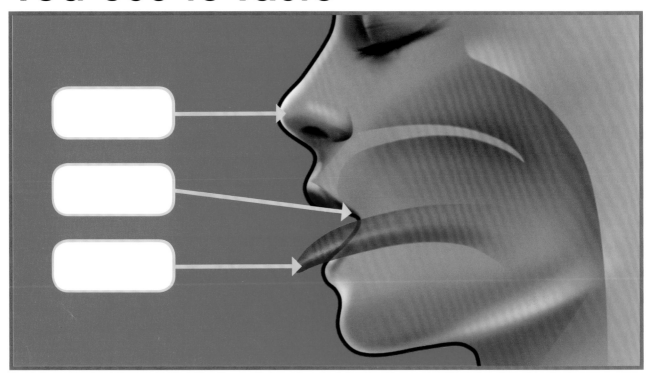

Point to where these labels should go.

nose   mouth   tongue

Answer on page 11.

Picture Glossary

flavor the taste and smell that something has

sense something that helps you smell, see, touch, taste, and hear things around you

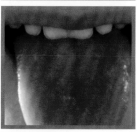

taste buds tiny parts on your tongue that help you to taste different things

umami meaty flavor

Index

flavors 15, 16, 17, 18, 19, 20, 21, 23

mouth 8, 11, 22

nose 10, 11, 22

senses 4, 5, 6, 7, 23

taste buds 12, 13, 23

tongue 9, 11, 12, 22

Note to Parents and Teachers
Before reading
Explain to children that people use five senses to understand the world: seeing, hearing, tasting, touching, and smelling. Tell children that there are different body parts associated with each sense. Then ask children which body parts they think they use to taste. Tell children that they use their mouth, tongue, and nose to taste flavors.

After reading
• Show children the diagram of the sensory system on page 22. Ask them to point to where the labels "mouth," "tongue," and "nose" should go.

• Write the five flavors on the board: salty, sweet, sour, bitter, umami. Then ask children to list foods that fall under each flavor category.

• Ask each child to write their favorite food on a small piece of paper. Then tape these pieces of paper on the board to form a bar chart of the classes favorite foods.